PRAIRIE GRASSLANDS

For Aubrey, with whom
I've shared all that matters
—W. L.

© NorthWord Books for Young Readers, 2006
Photography © 2006: Wayne Lynch
pp. 8 & 15 blazing star photos © Cliff Zenor
Map illustration by Mary Jo Scibetta
Designed by Lois A. Rainwater
Edited by Kristen McCurry

Books for Young Readers
11571 K-Tel Drive
Minnetonka, MN 55343
www.tnkidsbooks.com

Library of Congress Cataloging-in-Publication Data

Lynch, Wayne.
Prairie Grasslands / text and photographs by Wayne Lynch.
p. cm. -- (Our wild world ecosystems)
Includes index.
ISBN 1-55971-946-X (hardcover) -- ISBN 1-55971-947-8 (softcover)
1. Prairie ecology--United States--Juvenile literature. 2. Prairie ecology--Canada--Juvenile
literature. 3. Grassland ecology--United States--Juvenile literature.
4. Grassland ecology--Canada--Juvenile literature. I. Title.

QH104.L94 2006

577.4'4097--dc22   2005038016

Printed in Singapore
10 9 8 7 6 5 4 3 2

Our W**ILD** W**ORLD**™

ECOSYSTEMS

PRAIRIE GRASSLANDS

Text and Photographs by Wayne Lynch
Assisted by Aubrey Lang

NORTHWORD
Minnetonka, Minnesota

CONTENTS

"When I was a boy I loved to read books about wildlife, as I still do today. The first book I ever bought with my own money was *The Living Prairie.* It was a Walt Disney nature book with a photograph of a bison on the cover. I loved that book. I read it so often that the cover tore off and I had to tape the book together. Twenty-five years later, I finally visited the prairies, and they were as wonderful as I had dreamed they would be. It was June at the time. Golden bullsnakes warmed themselves in the summer sun, pronghorn fawns played in the waving grasses, and fast-flying falcons soared silently in the skies above me. In the prairies I felt at home. Today, after having photographed wildlife all over the world, the prairies are still my favorite place to be. Read on and you will learn why the prairies are so special to me."

A SEA OF GRASS

DID YOU KNOW THAT THERE ARE more than 9,000 different kinds of grass in the world besides the kind that grows on your front lawn? Grasses are found everywhere. There is even a kind of grass that grows in Antarctica, the coldest, driest, windiest, and iciest continent on Earth. In those parts of the world where there aren't many trees and where grasses are the main plants that cover the land, the area is called a grassland. This book is about the grasslands of North America, called the prairies.

THE GREAT PLAINS

The prairies in North America are also called the Great Plains—an immense sea of grass in the center of the continent. Early explorers called the Great Plains "a sea of grass" because when the wind blew, the swaying grasses reminded them of waves rolling across the ocean.

The Great Plains start in the eastern foothills of the Rocky Mountains and stretch, like a tabletop, more than 500 miles (805 km) east beyond the shores of the Mississippi River. In the south, the Great Plains begin in central Texas and go north all the way to Alberta and Saskatchewan in southern Canada. The Great Plains is a very big piece of prairie. If you tried to walk the whole length of it, walking nonstop day and night, it would take you more than a month!

Grasslands in different parts of the world have different names. In Asia grasslands are called steppes (STEPS). In southern Africa they are called veldts (VELTS), and in South America, pampas (POM-pahs).

(Left): The dried golden grass of winter contains very little nutrition and is not eaten by animals. (Inset Above): The spikes of red flowers on the prairie blazing star can grow up to 5 feet (1.5 m) tall.

This book is a different kind of nature book than you may have read before. It's a book about an ecosystem, the prairie ecosystem. An ecosystem is the word scientists use to describe all of the plants and animals that live together in a community and how these living things are affected by the richness of the soil, the warmth of the days, and the amount of rainfall that wets the land. In an ecosystem, all these things are connected, and all work together. The prairie ecosystem is a story about grass, sagebrush, and tumbleweeds. It's a story about hailstorms, winter blizzards, fire, lightning, and tornadoes. It's also a story about bison and burrowing owls, prairie dogs and rattlesnakes, and great noisy flocks of quacking ducks and geese.

SAGEBRUSH: a strong-smelling bush that grows in dry areas of the prairies

In the badlands, soft sandstone rocks can be shaped into strange forms called hoodoos.

CHAPTER TWO

I love to lie in the warm sunshine on the prairies and count the clouds while I run my fingers over the tops of the grass. Since I was a boy I've loved the taste of grass so I often chew on a stem and try to imagine what a deer or rabbit tastes when it does the same.

MORE THAN JUST GRASS!

GRASSES ARE SOME OF THE toughest plants in the world, and they can take just about whatever prairie weather and elements throw at them. You can crush them, bury them, break them, and even set them on fire, and they still survive. Grasses have flexible hollow stems that allow the plant to bend in the wind without breaking. When a grass plant is trampled, the side of the stem closest to the ground starts to grow and lifts the plant back up towards the sunlight. Look closely at a blade of grass and you can see that it has many tiny grooves on its surface. At the bottom of these grooves are the tiny holes through which the plant breathes. Because the holes are hidden in a groove they are protected from the drying effects of the wind and the grass loses less moisture. For this reason, grasses can live in areas where there is not much rain.

PRAIRIE SURVIVORS

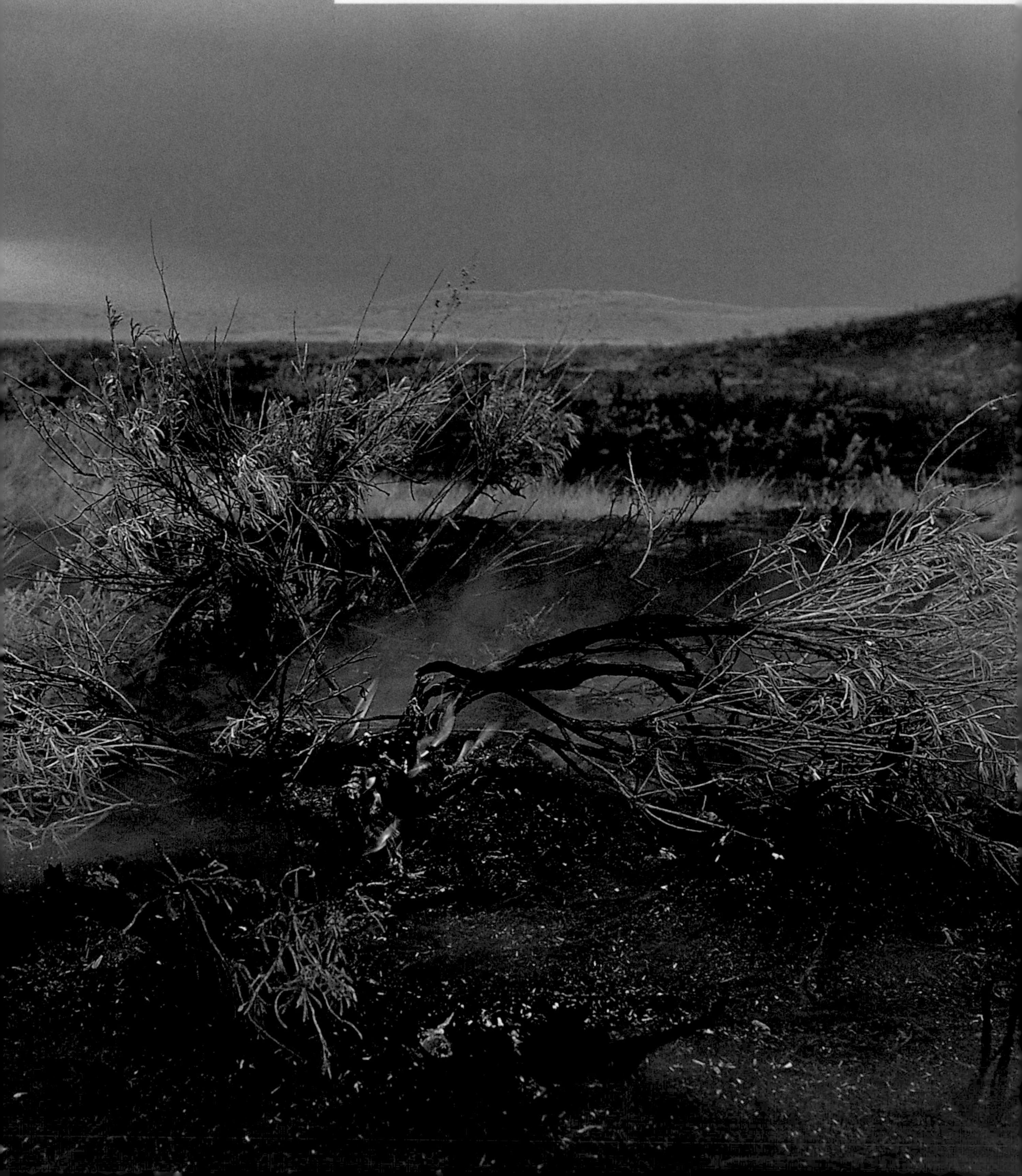

Grass leaves have a few other tricks to keep on waving. A blade of grass grows from its base, not from its tip, so a bison can nibble off most of a leaf and the plant will still survive. That's the reason you have to mow the grass on your lawn every few weeks—the leaves keep growing even though you keep cutting the ends off of them.

Most of the important growing parts of a grass plant are close to the ground or buried underneath it and this protects the grass from fire. Fires caused by lightning occur commonly in every grassland in the world, including the prairies. In earlier times, the Plains Indians often set the prairies on fire on purpose to help them when they were hunting and in times of war. They also burned the prairie to encourage fresh grass to grow, which they hoped would attract more bison. Because most prairie fires sweep across the ground quickly, the grasses are burned but not killed. The flames, however, do kill any bushes or trees trying to move into the prairies. You see, fire is a friend to prairie grasses because it keeps away other plants that would compete with them for water, soil, and sunlight.

One of the reasons grass is able to survive so well is that most of the plant is hidden underground. In fact, the biggest part of a grass plant is its roots. The thick roots of a grass plant hold the soil in place and keep it from blowing away. When the early pioneers moved to the prairies there was no wood to build their houses so they used blocks of earth that were held together by the thick roots of the grasses. These houses, called sod houses, usually had only one room in them and the walls were 2 feet (0.6 m) thick. Sod houses protected the people against the winter cold, the summer heat, and the year-round wind, but rain was a different story. The pioneers joked that if it rained outside for a day it would rain inside their house for two.

In a famous experiment done in the 1930s, a scientist discovered that a single plant of rye grass could grow 385 miles (620 km) of roots in just four months. When he also counted and measured all the tiny invisible hairs on the roots of that one plant, which it uses to soak up water and food, the total length of the roots was enough to stretch across the United States, twice!

FROM SHORT TO TALL

More than 300 different kinds of grass grow on the Great Plains of North America. If you look at a map of this area drawn by a scientist who studies grasses, you will see that the prairie is divided into three different sections. The tallgrass prairie forms the eastern edge of the Great Plains. Here, the grasses can grow up to 8 feet (2.4 m) tall! Early travelers wrote in their diaries that they could sometimes tie the tops of the grass over the saddle on their horses. The shortgrass prairie, which grows along the foothills of the Rocky Mountains, forms the western edge of the Great Plains. The grasses in this area rarely grow more than 2 feet (0.6 m) tall. Sandwiched between the shortgrass prairie in the west and the tallgrass prairie in the east is the largest slice of the Great Plains, the midgrass prairie. The grasses here grow 2 to 4 feet (0.6 to 1.2 m) tall. The boundaries between these three areas are not sharp and they blend together smoothly. Differences in rainfall explain why grasses grow taller in the east than in the west.

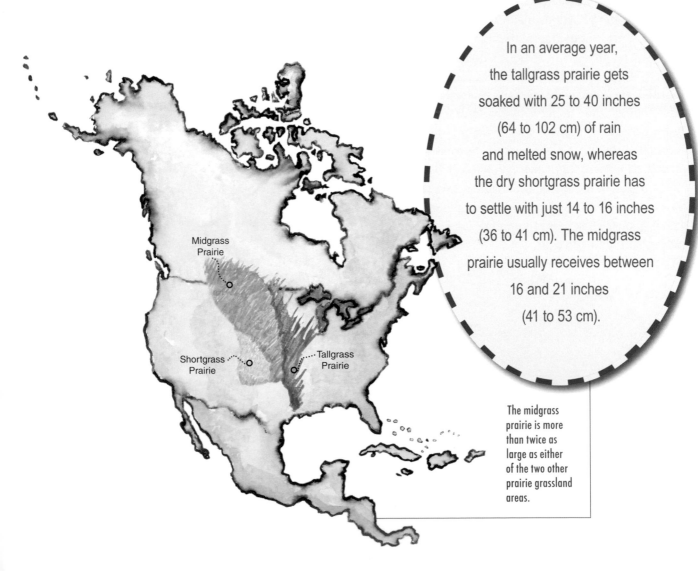

Midgrass Prairie

Shortgrass Prairie

Tallgrass Prairie

In an average year, the tallgrass prairie gets soaked with 25 to 40 inches (64 to 102 cm) of rain and melted snow, whereas the dry shortgrass prairie has to settle with just 14 to 16 inches (36 to 41 cm). The midgrass prairie usually receives between 16 and 21 inches (41 to 53 cm).

The midgrass prairie is more than twice as large as either of the two other prairie grassland areas.

Today, most of the tallgrass prairie is gone, plowed under and replaced by fields of corn. Although corn is also a grass, a cornfield has none of the wildlife richness found in a tallgrass prairie. The largest remaining area of tallgrass prairie is found in the Flint Hills of eastern Kansas. In most places, this part of the prairie survives only as tiny islands, sometimes no larger than a football field.

The midgrass prairie was less attractive to early farmers because it was drier and the soils were not as rich. Even so, only a third or more of the midgrass prairies survive today. In the rest, fields of wheat wave in the wind instead of wild grasses.

The shortgrass prairie, the driest of the three areas, has survived the best. More than half of it still exists. These days, the shortgrass prairies are used to raise cattle, but the native grasses and the wildlife can still be found.

ECO-Alert

Today, the farmer's plow is the biggest enemy of prairie grasslands. Every year, thousands of acres (hectares) of native prairie are destroyed by farmers hoping to grow more crops. Once the crops begin to grow, they are sprayed with many dangerous chemicals. Some are fertilizers to make the soil richer. Others are pesticides to kill harmful insects. And some are herbicides to kill weeds. All of these chemicals can harm wildlife, and sometimes even people as well.

TALLGRASS PRAIRIE

MIDGRASS PRAIRIE

SHORTGRASS PRAIRIE

PRAIRIE PRETTIES

Many different wildflowers add color and beauty to the green grass of the prairie. There are red blazing stars, purple coneflowers, scarlet pincushion cactuses, blue spiderworts, and yellow black-eyed Susans. Many of the flowers bloom in early spring when the ground is still wet from melted snow and water is plentiful. By blooming early they also get started before the grasses grow tall enough to shade them from the sunshine.

The beautiful yellow flowers of the golden-bean are poisonous, especially to children.

The crushed leaves of the scarlet globemallow were used by native people to treat skin wounds and blistered feet.

The western spiderwort grows well in sandy or rocky areas of the prairies.

Prickly pear and pincushion cactuses are well suited to grow in the heat and dryness of the western prairies. Their roots grow close to the surface to soak up the slightest rain shower, and their spines shade the plant and protect it from hungry animals.

I used to think that flowers were just pretty to look at but not very interesting to study. Then I discovered the secret life of the prairie crocus, one of the earliest flowers to bloom. To stay warm in early spring, the blossoms of the crocus follow the sun and face into it as it travels across the sky throughout the day. The petals of these flowers are shaped like saucers, which focus the sun's rays into the center of the blossom, raising its temperature. This speeds up the growth of the flower's seeds. The warmer temperatures also attract tiny beetles and other insects, which come to heat themselves and then accidentally help spread pollen. Who would have thought that a flower could be such a clever heat-seeking saucer?

The prairie crocus is one of the earliest wildflowers to bloom in spring. Its hairy stems and leaves protect it from the cold temperatures.

SNOW-EATERS
AND GOLF BALLS OF ICE

The amount of rain and snow that falls on a prairie not only determines whether grasses are tall or short, but also whether a grassland exists at all. If an area receives less rain than a shortgrass prairie it becomes a desert. If it receives more than a tallgrass prairie it becomes a forest. Over time, the climate of the world has changed many times. When this happens, deserts sometimes become grasslands, and grasslands often become forests. As the world now heats up with global warming, rainfall patterns will certainly change again, and some grasslands in North America will eventually become deserts.

The climate of the prairies depends upon more than rainfall and snow; it also depends upon the temperature. Because the Great Plains are in the center of the continent, far from the Atlantic and Pacific Oceans, they are often extremely cold in winter, and extremely hot in summer. If the oceans were closer to the prairies, their waters would keep the grasslands warmer in winter and cooler in summer. But the added moisture would allow trees and other plants to grow, overtaking the prairie grasses.

CLIMATE: the different types of weather that occur in an area

GLOBAL WARMING: heating of Earth's atmosphere from the burning of large amounts of gasoline, coal, and natural gas

This violent hailstorm on the Canadian prairies lasted less than 30 minutes. Hail the size of gravel flattened the grasses.

Compare the temperatures and conditions in prairie Kansas with those on the coast of California next to the warm Pacific Ocean. In Kansas, when there is a winter blizzard with freezing cold and blowing snow, it may be mild and raining on the coast of California. In the middle of summer there is also a big difference between the two areas because of the ocean. Kansas often bakes in temperatures over 90°F (32°C), enduring violent thunderstorms and tornadoes. On the coast of California, temperatures are in the 70s and 80s F (20s C), and there is often a cool, fresh breeze from the ocean.

It's the warm summer temperatures, the wind, and the dryness of the Great Plains that create the perfect conditions for prairie grasses to grow.

Winds are a big part of life on the prairies. Cowboys often joke that they never get upset if they lose their hat to a gusty prairie wind. They simply sit down for a while and grab the next hat that blows by. In winter, warm dry winds, called *Chinooks*, often sweep down the eastern side of the Rocky Mountains and across the prairies. Chinook is a Native American word meaning "snow-eater," and these warm winds can raise the temperature by many degrees in a matter of minutes and melt the snow. In less than an hour a Chinook can change the weather from winter to spring.

The warm winds are usually strongest near the mountains, and gradually lessen as you move east. Chinooks also occur in the Black Hills of South Dakota, which hold the record for the fastest rise in temperature ever recorded. In January 1943, the temperature rose 49°F (9°C) in just two minutes! The snow-eating temperatures persisted for several hours, then suddenly fell again to -4°F (-20°C).

Summer in the prairies is when the weather can be most dangerous. Violent thunderstorms are common, and the tall black clouds sometimes produce deadly tornadoes. Tornadoes are funnel-shaped clouds spinning at 300 miles per hour (483 kph) or more. Tornadoes can be very powerful, and strong enough to lift railway cars off their tracks. Once, when a tornado destroyed a schoolhouse with 85 children inside, the swirling funnel cloud carried some of the students the length of a football field before dropping them. Amazingly, all of the children survived.

Severe thunderstorms can also produce damaging hail. Hailstorms are most feared by farmers because they can flatten and destroy their

A warm chinook wind can melt the snow covering the badlands in a single day.

Texas, Oklahoma, Kansas, and Nebraska get hit by the most prairie tornadoes, although they can occur anywhere in the Great Plains. In some years, more than 150 tornadoes swirl across Texas.

crops in just a couple of minutes. To protect themselves, prairie farmers together spend millions of dollars on hail insurance every year.

Hailstones the size of golf balls are not uncommon in the prairies, but the largest hailstone ever recorded fell with a thud on Aurora, Nebraska, in June 2003. The jagged chunk of ice was as large as a volleyball and may have weighed more than 1.5 pounds (0.7 kg) before it broke apart! A piece of ice that big could easily kill a person if it hit them, but only two people in North America have ever been killed by hailstones in the last 100 years.

Not surprisingly, hailstorms can also be dangerous to animals and birds. In 1978, in Montana, hailstones the size of baseballs killed 200 sheep. In Alberta, a hailstorm in 1953 killed 36,000 ducks. A second storm struck the same area a few days later and killed another 30,000 quackers. No one knows how many songbirds and other small animals died in the storm as well.

All of these conditions, though sometimes harsh, are what build the prairies and create homes for prairie wildlife. Besides the rolling prairies, which earned the "sea of grass" nickname, there are three other prairie habitats, or places where wildlife live: wetlands circled by cattails and bulrushes; badlands filled with rocks and caves; and river valleys crowded with trees and bushes.

All kinds of critters, roamers, hoppers, and fliers can be found in each of these habitats. Some prairie animals may live their entire lives in just one of these four habitats, such as waterbirds in the wetlands. Others, **HABITAT:** the natural home where an animal lives such as the coyote, may wander through each habitat. Wildlife is the part of nature that interests me most and that's what we'll talk about next. In this book the animals are grouped according to their most common habitats, but many can also be found in other areas of the prairie.

CHAPTER THREE

It was early April and I hoped to photograph the spring courtship dances of the prairie sage grouse. I had slept in a sleeping bag beside my photo blind on the ground. When I woke up just before sunrise, my face was cold and the grass around me was covered with frost. Already I could hear the sage grouse calling and the sound made me forget the cold and the ache in my back. I carefully crawled inside my blind and looked through the telephoto lens of my camera. There, in the golden light of dawn, were a dozen splendid male sage grouse strutting and calling together. Each wanted to attract a mate. For thousands of years these magnificent prairie birds had suffered through long prairie winters, blizzards, droughts, hailstorms, and tornadoes. These were the survivors and I felt privileged to watch them.

PHOTO BLIND: a small square tent that photographers use to hide from wildlife

TELEPHOTO: a special camera lens that makes animals look closer than they really are

ROLLING GRASSLANDS

WHEN MOST PEOPLE THINK of the prairies they think of gently rolling grasslands. It is the largest wildlife habitat in the Great Plains. Here, fast-footed pronghorn race their shadows against the wind, handsome male prairie chickens strut and cluck, and songbirds make beautiful music high in the sky. The rolling grasslands are "big sky" country. Without trees to block the view, you can watch a parade of clouds sweep overhead and melt away in the distance.

BISON BATTLES

Perhaps 30 million bison once roamed the Great Plains—roughly the same number as the current human population of Canada. The great herds of bellowing bison, often called buffalo, were sometimes so large that they took days to move through a valley, and they wandered great distances in a year. Weary bison hunters sometimes joked that the big shaggy beasts like to have breakfast in Texas, dinner in Oklahoma, and supper in Kansas. Today, there are about 450,000 bison in the United States, most of them inside fences on private ranches. Very few bison are wild and free.

The bison is the largest animal in North America. A large bull bison weighs as much as a small car. The animals are most exciting to watch

Dr. Dale Lott, a bison expert, describes the bellow of a bull bison as "equal parts lion roar and thunderclap that booms across the grass."

during the mating season in late July and early August when bulls fight and bang heads together like woolly battering rams. The battles often begin with bellowing.

Bulls bellow to challenge other bulls, and their roars carry for miles (km) across the flat, treeless prairies. Once the bulls lock horns they push and shove with all their strength and clouds of dust swirl around them. If one of the fighters surrenders and runs, he usually escapes without any injury. Sometimes, though, if a bull stumbles or falls, the other bull may attack. Then, ribs can be broken, muscles bruised, and bodies bloodied. When the mating season is finally over, the weary bulls spend the days of autumn gaining weight for the long, cold months of winter that lie ahead.

ECO-Fact

If you look closely at dried cow manure you can see many tiny bits of grass in it. The early settlers on the prairies gathered wagonloads of dry bison manure, called "buffalo chips," to burn in their stoves instead of wood. Buffalo chips were free, they burned slowly and hot, and the smoke smelled like grass.

MANURE: animal droppings

In the rolling grasslands there are very few trees. This can be a problem when you are a bird. First, there are no treetops from which to sing. Second, there are no leafy branches where you can safely hide your nest. Birds in the grasslands have solved these problems in interesting ways.

Male birds sing to attract females and frighten away other males. To do this well, they need to sing from a perch where they can be clearly heard. Since there are no trees to help them out, they sing in flight. Horned larks, pipits, longspurs, and lark buntings all sing beautiful songs while they float and flutter high in the sky. The Sprague's pipit, a plain small brown bird, may circle in the sky for an hour or more, almost out of sight, singing its delicate jingle over and over again.

The crow-sized long-billed curlew has a bill that is 9 inches (23 cm) long.

Like many prairie birds, the upland sandpiper sings on the wing while circling high in the sky.

The shortage of trees also affects where grassland birds must build their nests, so many of them nest on the ground. The nests of curlews, killdeers, sparrows, larks, and many others are either a simple dip in the ground with nothing added to it, or a small grassy cup lined with feathers and hair. To hide from predators, most birds that nest on the ground are brown or gray in color and their backs are streaked and spotted to blend perfectly with the grasses around them. Their eggs are also camouflaged (CAM-uh-flaashzd) to hide them when the parents are away from the nest. Many predators in the prairies hunt for birds that nest on the ground, including skunks, coyotes, red foxes, magpies, crows, and bull snakes.

CAMOUFLAGE: a pattern or color that makes an animal or egg blend with its background

PREDATOR: an animal that hunts and kills other animals

ECO-Fact

In the past, the brown-headed cowbird was called the buffalo bird because it followed the migrating herds of bison and fed on the insects they stirred up. But this presented a problem. How could the birds stay with the moving herds and still feed hungry youngsters in a nest? The solution for the cowbird was to lay its eggs in other birds' nests so it could continue to follow the bison. The foster parents unknowingly raised the cowbird's chicks. Today, we know that a female cowbird may lay 40 eggs in a season, all in different nests.

MIGRATE: when an animal or bird moves to a new area for the winter

This hungry coyote was hunting for voles and mice tunneling through the deep grass. The crafty coyote caught two voles in just a couple of minutes.

One time when I planned to photograph the five fuzzy-headed chicks in a meadowlark's nest I got a big surprise. As I moved the grasses away from the top of the nest for a closer look I froze in fear. The head of a large prairie rattlesnake rested on the edge of the nest, inches (cm) from my hand. The snake's body was swollen and had several bulges in it. The snake had probably swallowed the entire family of fuzzies without wasting a single drop of venom. I thought, if a snake can smile, this one had good reason to.

Next to the bison, if I were to choose one animal to be the symbol of the grasslands it would be the black-tailed prairie dog. Early explorers to the prairies were amazed by the great numbers of prairie dogs that lived in huge "dogtowns" all across the Great Plains. In Texas in the 1800s, there was a prairie dog colony that measured 100 miles by 250 miles (161 by 402 km). That's bigger than the combined states of Connecticut, Delaware, Maryland, and New Jersey! Imagine an area that big filled with 400 million noisy, barking ground squirrels and you have some idea what early travelers saw. Today, after a hundred years of poisons, steel traps, and plows, the black-tailed prairie dog population is less than two percent of what it once was.

In the dogtowns that still exist, life goes on much as it always did. The burrows that prairie dogs dig and the way they clip the grass short in their colonies attracts many other prairie animals and birds. In Oklahoma, scientists counted 56 species (SPEE-sees) of birds, 18 species of mammals, 10 different kinds of snakes and lizards, and 7 different toads and frogs, all using prairie dog towns. Black-footed ferrets, long-tailed weasels, and badgers do more than use the burrows in a prairie dog town—they also eat the prairie dogs for breakfast, lunch, and dinner whenever they can. The only defense the squirrels have is to bark a warning, then dive underground

The American badger is a real digging machine. It has strong muscles and claws that are 3 inches (7.6 cm) long.

nest chamber with dried, shredded cattle or horse manure. Some scientists believe the strong smell of the manure covers up the odor of the owl and hides the tricky bird from sharp-nosed predators such as badgers, foxes, and ferrets. The manure may also attract dung beetles, which the owls can eat as a handy snack. If you remove the manure, as I once did as an experiment, the owls replace it within two days.

and hide in one of their many tunnels. Sometimes, if they are feeling especially brave, they may plug a tunnel where a predator has gone, but mostly they just run and hide.

When a prairie dog deserts a burrow, a skunk may move in, or a bull snake, or a cottontail rabbit. One grassland house-hunter that often uses old prairie dog burrows is the 10-inch- (25-cm-) tall burrowing owl. The owls have the unusual habit of lining the tunnel and

ECO-Alert

The burrowing owl is declining in both the United States and Canada. Scientists are uncertain why this is happening. Pesticides and the loss of prairie lands may be to blame. Also, many of these owls spend the winter in Mexico where they may face problems we don't know about yet.

PRAIRIE DANCERS

Four different species of grouse (greater sage grouse, greater prairie chicken, lesser prairie chicken, and sharp-tailed grouse) strut and dance on different areas of the prairies in springtime. All of them gather at special dancing grounds, called *leks*, where the males puff themselves up, coo and cluck, and show off for any females in sight. Forty or 50 males may dance together on the same lek, which may be half the size of an Olympic-sized swimming pool.

The male greater sage grouse at the right is surrounded by at least nine females with whom he will mate. The male sharp-tailed grouse below has attracted no females to his dancing grounds.

The males in the center of a lek are always the oldest, healthiest birds. These are the birds that the females usually want to mate with them. Most of the males on the edges of the lek are younger birds with no experience. They usually do nothing but practice their dancing and watch the lucky winners in the center of the lek.

All of the female grouse are single mothers. After the males mate with them, the females leave the lek and lay their eggs. When the eggs hatch, the mothers raise their chicks alone.

The Plains Indians knew the different grouse well, and they liked to copy the birds in their dances and costumes. They also hunted the grouse on their leks. Some leks have been used by grouse for over a hundred years so they are often a good place to look for old Indian arrowheads.

ARROWHEADS:
the stone and bone points
that native people
wrapped on the tips of their
arrows and spears

When I think of pronghorn, I think of speed. After all, it's the fastest mammal in North America. It can race at 60 miles per hour (100 kph), and keep up that speed for several miles (km). What might be even more interesting to think about is *why* is the pronghorn such a speedster? So that they can escape from predators? Perhaps long ago they had to run for their lives, but there are no predators on the prairies today that run fast enough to catch a pronghorn. Pronghorn expert Dr. John Byers believes that pronghorns are fast because they are running away from the ghosts of past predators.

The pronghorn has been racing over the prairies of North America for nearly four million years. Up until just 10,000 years ago, there were many fleet-footed predators chasing pronghorn across the Great Plains for a meal. There was the American lion, which was a larger, faster version of the cat that now lives in Africa. There was also the American hunting hyena with bone-crushing teeth, and the giant short-faced bear that stood as tall as a man's shoulders and ran as fast as a horse. However, the two most dangerous predators for a pronghorn in those times were two species of cheetahs, both of which were fast-running cats. All of these predators eventually disappeared from the North American prairies, but the pronghorn did not. It seems the sagebrush speedster is still running from the memory of those predators.

A newborn pronghorn hides in the prairie grasses by curling into a ball and staying perfectly still.

CHAPTER FOUR

I've always thought the horned grebe (GREEB) was a really cool prairie bird. It has bright red eyes and golden feathers along the sides of its head that it can raise into fluffy horns when it gets excited. The grebe builds a floating nest in deep water and the first time I tried to photograph one I learned a painful lesson.

One day I forgot my tall rubber boots so I decided to go barefoot and just stand in the mud inside my photo blind. It was a hot day and the mud was nice and cool. That day I forgot something else besides my boots. I forgot that leeches, bloodworms, and other hungry creepy crawlies live in prairie mud. When my bare feet squished into the goo I didn't realize that I was ringing the dinner bell for the munchkins in the mud. At the time, I didn't feel anything biting my feet and ankles. The surprise came later. That night, I had red spots and bubbles all over the skin of my legs and feet, and the itch was terrible. I scratched for a week.

WETLANDS

WATER IS IMPORTANT TO WILDLIFE everywhere, but there are not many lakes on the prairies. Instead, there are potholes and playas (PLY-yahs), which are similar to shallow ponds. Potholes tend to hold more water and occur mostly in the northern prairies of North Dakota, South Dakota, Minnesota, and Canada. Playas are most common in the southern prairies of Texas, Oklahoma, Colorado, and Kansas.

Playas and potholes are different than lakes. They have no rivers or streams running into them or out of them, and they receive all their water from melting snow and rainfall that drains from the surrounding prairies. Because of this, most prairie wetlands are quite shallow, and many of them dry up in summer.

PLAYAS AND POTHOLES

Playas and potholes may not be deep, or last a long time, but they still have great value. Their waters are rich in minerals and plant food that get washed in from the surrounding grasslands. This produces the perfect growing conditions for duckweeds, pondweeds, diving beetles, snails, bloodworms, leeches, water bears, and many other tiny aquatic plants and animals. Because of their richness, potholes and playas are vital to prairie wildlife. Frogs, toads, and salamanders visit them to lay their eggs. Arctic-nesting ducks, geese, swans, and shorebirds stop at them in spring and autumn to rest, eat, and build up extra fat. Blackbirds, wrens, night herons, bitterns, and

The tiger salamander is commonly found in prairie potholes where it hunts insects, frogs, worms, and other salamanders.

grebes nest in the safety of their cattails, and mink and raccoons hunt along their shorelines. More than all of this, potholes are especially important to ducks that nest on the prairies—so important, that scientists call the potholes of the northern prairies the "Duck Factory of North America." This is because half of all the ducks in Canada and the United States start life there.

ECO-Fact

The northern harrier is the most common hawk that hunts in the cattails around prairie potholes. Unlike most other hawks, the harrier uses its hearing, just like many owls do, to capture mice and voles.

Unlike most hawks in which the males and females look alike, the male northern harrier pictured here is gray in color and the female is dark brown.

VOLE: a small mouse-sized animal with a stubby tail

DEVIL DIVERS AND WATER WITCHES

Six species of grebes live in the wetlands of the prairies. Grebes are waterbirds that look like ducks, but they are altogether different. Whereas a duck's bill is blunt and flattened for sifting through mud and plant material, a grebe's bill is slim and pointed for feeding on aquatic beetles, worms, tadpoles, and tiger salamanders. All grebes are expert divers, but their legs are so far

A grebe can disappear underwater without a ripple, and the astonishing speed with which they can do this has earned them colorful nicknames like "devil diver" and "water witch."

to the rear of their bodies that if they tried to walk on land like a duck does they would tip over onto their head.

If I were an egg, the best place to be would be in a duck's nest. The worst place would be in a grebe's nest. In a duck's nest, I would always be dry and cradled in fluffy, warm feathers. In a grebe's nest, I would always be wet and dirty. Luckily, the grebes don't seem to mind. All grebes build floating nests made of rotting water plants, and their eggs often sit in water. Grebe eggs are white when they are first laid, but they soon become stained brown from the decaying nest. The best part of being a grubby grebe egg is that when you hatch, you get to ride on your parent's back, something that no spoiled baby duck ever gets to do.

DIVERS AND DABBLERS

Ducks are some of my favorite prairie birds, but the many different kinds can sometimes be hard to tell apart. Many years ago, I learned a little trick that helped me sort them out. Prairie ducks can be divided into two groups: divers and dabblers. Watching how a particular duck feeds, and how it flies away, will help you tell the two groups apart.

The diving ducks, which include the canvasback, redhead, and ruddy duck, usually stay in the deeper water in the middle of a pothole or playa, and disappear completely when they search for food underwater. The dabblers, which include the mallard, blue-winged teal, gadwall, and northern shoveler, usually paddle along in the shallows at the edge of a pothole and skim food off the top of the water. They may also tip their bottoms up to reach food just below the surface.

If you accidentally frighten the ducks in a prairie pothole you can tell whether they are divers or dabblers just by watching the way they fly away. A dabbler jumps straight into the air and flies off. A diver, on the other hand, must run across the surface of the water to build up speed before it can take off.

When it comes time to build a nest, the divers and dabblers are different again. The dabblers build their nests away from the water. They may waddle up to 2 miles (3.2 km) away and hide their nests on the ground in the thick grasses beside roadways, along fences, or under bushes. Because the diving ducks are clumsy walkers, they prefer to stay close to the water. They build their nests in the bulrushes and cattails around the edges of a pothole.

ECO-Alert

Potholes and playas are often drained to make more room for crops. Without these valuable wetlands, ducks, geese, and other prairie waterbirds have no place to nest and raise their young. An organization called Ducks Unlimited tries to convince farmers and other landowners to protect wetlands for the future.

A FROGGY WENT A-COURTING

Frogs and toads are usually pretty quiet, until it's time to mate. Then, they become real loudmouths. The males are the ones who make all the noise. Each singer calls from his own tiny territory along the edge of the water. A male frog or toad may sing a thousand times in a night, and he does this to win the heart of a lady.

Just like birds, every species of frog and toad sings a different song. The ears of a female frog are most sensitive to the sound of her own species. She hears this best, even when six or seven different types of frogs and toads may be singing loudly at the same time. A similar thing happens when you are in a crowded room and your mother calls your name. You hear her voice immediately even if the room is full of talking people.

Because so many prairie potholes and playas dry up in the summer, prairie frogs and toads need to lay their eggs as quickly as they can. Once the males start calling, the females soon arrive. Then the

choosing begins. A female toad may have hundreds of males she can choose as her mate, but she's probably looking for a winner. She likely wants a partner that is healthy and has lived long enough to prove that he can feed himself well and avoid predators. These are the good qualities a female toad wants to pass on to her toadlets.

So how does she pick a winner? Scientists don't know for sure, but they think she probably listens closely to his voice. Older, healthy males may sing louder and more often than younger, weak males. In some species of frogs, older males also sing faster than young ones. As it turns out, female frogs seem to prefer fast talkers.

All dragonflies, such as this variable darner, have huge eyes that are very sensitive to motion and help them catch insects in flight.

ECO-Fact

Colorful dragonflies are common in many prairie wetlands. They have wonderful names such as cherry-faced meadowhawk, four-spotted skimmer, and pale snaketail. All of them are fast-flying insect killers. They especially like to hunt mosquitoes. A hungry dragonfly may eat 300 of them in a day, earning the nickname mosquito hawk.

CHAPTER FIVE

Whenever I find an old animal burrow in the prairies I always take a closer look to check for critters. Sometimes I discover a sunbathing rattlesnake, a lizard, or a toad. My favorite animal to find is the black widow spider. One day when I peeked inside an old ground squirrel burrow I found a female black widow that was bigger than usual. I knew it was a female because it was a shiny black color with a large red patch on the belly. I decided to take her back to my campsite to photograph. I had an empty glass peanut butter jar in my truck and I used that to trap the venomous lady. I knew that prairie black widow spiders were dangerous but not deadly, and as far as I could remember, no healthy adult had ever died from their bite. But I didn't want to be the first.

The next day, it was time to photograph my new pet. Overnight, the spider had spun a messy web under the lid of the jar and she seemed to have shrunk. I wondered what had happened. Maybe she was dying? Then, in the corner of the jar, I noticed a pea-sized ball of yellow silk. It was an egg case. The black widow had been pregnant when I caught her and overnight she had laid her eggs and wrapped them carefully in silk. Inside the sac there were probably 200 eggs.

After taking some photos I drove back to the badlands where I had captured the spider and returned her and her sac of eggs to the burrow where I had found them. All wildlife deserves the right to live and I wanted the spider and her family to have that chance.

BADLANDS

MOST OF THE PRAIRIES ARE either flat, or gently rolling like the smooth surface of the ocean. There is one area of the prairies, however, that is all up and down. It is called the badlands. This is a land of barren slopes, and steep, narrow valleys. Few plants grow on the bare soil, so a visitor can easily see the different layers of rock, like the layers in a slice of cake. Prairie grasses still find a chance to grow, though, here and there on the slopes and in the valleys between the slopes.

Famous badlands are found
along the Missouri River in Montana,
in Badlands National Park in South Dakota,
and along the Red Deer River
and Milk River in southern Alberta.

No one is certain where the name badlands comes from. Some people believe that the early trappers were the first to name them because they found these areas difficult to travel through. Others think that the first settlers gave them their name when they found the rocky badlands impossible to plow. Whichever you believe, the badlands are still only "bad" from the viewpoint of humans. For prairie wildlife they are a place to hide and flourish. For the nature lover, they are a place of beauty and wild secrets.

The badlands are different from the surrounding prairies because of something that happened 15,000 years ago. That was when the huge glaciers of the Ice Age began to melt and pour great rivers of water over the northern prairies. Continually running water is strong enough to eat through rock, and that is what happened. The meltwater from the glaciers carved deep valleys in the land. Once the ice had melted, the rivers dried up, and the land drained. The badlands were born.

GLACIER:
a slow-moving river of ice

MELTWATER:
water formed by the melting of ice or snow

Today, rainwater, wind, and freezing temperatures continue to carve tiny bits of rock from the surface of the badlands, year after year. What remains are caves and crevices, and interesting mushroom-shaped hoodoos, a symbol of the badlands. On a moonlit night, the hoodoos can produce long, spooky shadows. The Blackfoot Indians were frightened of hoodoos, and thought they were giants of stone who came alive at night and threw rocks at anyone who dared to visit.

HOODOO:
a mushroom-shaped rock formed by rainwater and repeated freezing and warming

ECO-Fact

Dinosaur Provincial Park in the badlands of Alberta is one of the most important dinosaur fossil locations in the world. The barren rocky slopes make it easier for the scientists to find the buried bones. So far, they have discovered fossils from 36 different kinds of dinosaurs, as well as from 80 kinds of fish, frogs, turtles, crocodiles, and primitive mammals.

Scientists aren't really sure how rattlesnakes got the noisy rattle at the end of their tail. They think long ago the snakes' ancestors may have grown it to attract the attention of large animals like deer, elk, and bison, which have heavy, sharp hooves. By warning these animals that they were nearby, the snakes didn't get accidentally stepped on and injured or killed.

The bull snake is a rattlesnake copycat. Its coloration is similar to a rattler, and it buzzes its tail to frighten predators away like a rattlesnake does.

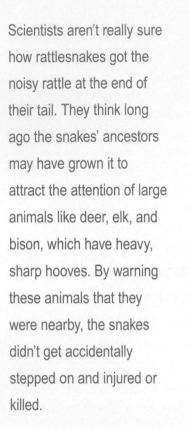

In the winter, freezing temperatures occur across most of the prairies. Snakes die when they freeze, so prairie snakes must escape underground for the winter. The deep cracks and caves in the badlands are a good place for snakes to flee. Different kinds of snakes may spend the winter together. I once found a snake den where there were garter snakes, yellow-bellied racers, bull snakes, and prairie rattlesnakes all spending the winter together in the same crevice. A rattlesnake doesn't eat other snakes, so they are safe around this venomous hunter.

Rattlesnakes have a special power different from other prairie snakes. They can feel the body heat of warm-blooded animals on their face. The snakes have a small pit between each eye and at the end of their nose. Just as you could tell the direction of a fireplace from the heat you feel on your face, even if you were blindfolded, a rattlesnake can locate mice, voles, and ground squirrels in complete darkness by detecting the heat from their bodies.

HUNTING WINGS

Most hawks, eagles, falcons, vultures, and owls are shy and easily bothered, especially when they are nesting and raising chicks. The secret hidden cliffs, ledges, and holes of the badlands are a perfect place for these birds to hunt and hide. Here, they can find a safe nesting place, lots of food, and few people to upset them. More species of hunting birds, called raptors (RAP-tors) or birds of prey, nest in the badlands than in any other area of the prairies. In some parts of the badlands you may see golden eagles, ferruginous (fur-OO-jin-us) hawks, merlins, kestrels, prairie falcons, turkey vultures, and great horned owls.

PREY: an animal that is hunted and killed by another animal for food

With so many different raptors living together in the badlands, how do the birds keep from competing with each other? They do it by nesting in different places and hunting different prey.

Golden eagles are the biggest badland raptors and have their pick of the largest prey, including cottontail rabbits, jackrabbits, sharp-tailed grouse, and pheasants. Ferruginous hawks and great horned owls are next in line, size-wise, and large enough to hunt many of the same animals. Great horned owls, however, nest differently. While the hawks and eagles build big, bulky stick nests on

The majestic golden eagle may raise one to three chicks depending upon how much food there is. When food is scarce the largest eagle chick may kill its smaller brother or sister.

high cliff ledges, the great horned owl never builds a nest of its own. It either takes over a deserted nest of a crow or a hawk, or it squeezes into a hole in the cliffs. The great horned owl also avoids competition by hunting at night instead of during the day.

The turkey vulture is also a big bird, but it's mostly feathers and not much muscle. The bare rock inside a cave makes a fine nest for the vulture, and a dead animal of any size makes a delicious dinner.

The three falcons, the small-sized kestrel, the medium-sized merlin, and the large prairie falcon also divide up the badlands so that they don't get in each other's way. The small kestrel eats mainly grasshoppers, beetles, crickets, and spiders, and it nests inside the smallest holes it can find in the cliffs. The merlin hunts songbirds of any size and often nests in abandoned magpie nests. The prairie falcon hunts ground squirrels as well as mourning doves and larks. This fast-flying falcon commonly nests on barren ledges or inside holes in the face of a cliff.

ECO-Alert

Many eagles, hawks, and falcons that live in the badlands are easily upset if someone approaches their nest too closely. Sometimes the shy birds will desert their eggs or chicks after just one visit by a person. Today, more and more people like to hike in the beautiful wilderness of the badlands. Educating them not to disturb such birds is an important step to take.

The six-week-old great horned owl chick above had just left the family nest, as had the young ferruginous hawk on the right. The hawk was guarding a meal that its parents had brought to it.

HIDERS
AND RUNNERS

The grasslands are home to five different animals belonging to the rabbit and hare family. They are the white-tailed jackrabbit, black-tailed jackrabbit, eastern cottontail, desert cottontail, and mountain cottontail. Which are which? The jackrabbits are hares, and the cottontails are rabbits, and there is a big difference between them.

Rabbits are hiders. They depend greatly on holes. They use them to escape from predators and also to give birth to their young. Pregnant mother rabbits make a nest of grass inside a deep hole and line it with fur that they pluck from their belly and sides. Newborn rabbits, called kittens, are born blind, naked, and helpless.

Hares are quite different. When a hare is chased by a predator, the hare doesn't hide like a rabbit, it runs for its life. Some speedy jackrabbits can sprint at 45 miles per hour (72 kph). On the prairies, only the pronghorn is faster.

Mother hares also raise their babies differently. They give birth to them out in the open, on top of the ground. The newborn hares, called leverets, are fully furred, their eyes are open, and they are ready to hip-hop away as soon as they are born.

There's one final difference between rabbits and hares. Most rabbits live in southern areas where winters are short and mild, and most hares live in the north where winters are long and snowy. As a result, many hares turn white in winter, including the white-tailed jackrabbit, to help them hide from predators. Rabbits, which always hide in holes, don't need camouflage and stay brown all year round.

Both the Nuttall's cottontail on the left and the white-tailed jackrabbit below were photographed in winter. You can see that the jackrabbit turns white in winter and the cottontail does not.

CHAPTER SIX

As a wildlife photographer I get to spy on the secret lives of many animals and birds. One spring I spent three and a half months watching a family of great horned owls raise their chicks. I built a platform in a tree about 30 feet (9 m) off the ground. At that height, I could look right into the nest and see everything that was happening. I watched the chicks grow from blind, fluffy balls of white fuzz into bold, beautiful owls. I giggled as they bobbed their heads back and forth to watch a woodpecker tapping in a tree next to their nest. The wobbly chicks made me laugh out loud when they tumbled over watching a plane fly overhead.

After a late snowstorm in spring, they left the nest. I followed their tracks in the snow and found them hiding safely in the woods, perched on fallen trees. It was a spring I will never forget, and even as I write these words I laugh at the wonderful memories I have of those three little owls.

RIVER VALLEYS

NATURALLY, MOST OF THE GRASSLANDS are covered with grass, but that doesn't mean there are no trees. Along the eastern edge of the tallgrass prairie, oak trees of different species continually try to invade the prairies. Periodic fires keep them from winning very often. Along the western edge of the grasslands, in the foothills of the Rocky Mountains, ponderosa pines and aspen poplars creep into the prairies wherever they can find enough water to satisfy their thirst. Both edges of the prairies are like battlefields where grasses and trees continually fight to conquer each other. Fire, rainfall, and summer heat decide which will win and which will lose.

Many great rivers cross the width of the prairies, including the South Saskatchewan, Missouri, Platte, Arkansas, and Canadian Rivers. Because the prairies are so flat, all of these rivers flow slowly along, often looping back and forth as they go. None of them has dangerous rapids and waterfalls. The rivers are perfect places to drift peacefully with a canoe on a summer afternoon.

One place in the prairies where trees are often the winner is along the river valleys. The valleys are shaded and cooler than the open prairies. The ground is usually more moist and resistant to fire than on the grasslands, and the rivers that flow through the valleys are a handy source of water for thirsty cottonwoods, elms, and oaks.

The trees along the river valleys are like fingers of forest that stretch across the prairies. They connect the forests in the east with the forests in the west.

ECO-Fact

You would think that nothing would be brave enough to eat a smelly skunk or prickly porcupine. The great horned owl eats both of them, but not without a risk. Skunk-hunting owls often get sprayed and one unlucky owl that scientists examined had 84 porcupine quills in its face, sides, and legs. Ouch.

Many prairie animals and birds use river valleys as travel corridors. When this happens, birds from the east may meet similar species from the west. Lazuli (LAZ-you-lie) buntings from the west run into indigo (IN-dee-go) buntings from the east, western black-headed grosbeaks join up with eastern rose-breasted grosbeaks, and western Bullock's orioles meet eastern Baltimore orioles.

In total, river valley forests cover just a small part of the prairies, but they are vital to its wildlife richness. Half of all the birds living in the prairies are found in these small forests. Prairie forests are also important areas for bobcats to bound, porcupines to prickle, coyotes to yodel, and bats to flutter.

The bobcat is about twice as large as an average housecat. It hunts in river valleys for birds, small mammals, snakes, and frogs.

TICK TALK

Ticks are blood-sucking creepy crawlies. They are related to spiders and they resemble tiny watermelon seeds with eight legs. Two kinds of ticks are common in the prairies: the dog tick and the Rocky Mountain wood tick. Both are found around bushes in river valleys. Knowing a little about what makes a tick "tick" may make it less scary.

Adult ticks, the usual ones that bite people, are most active in the spring. They climb to the top of a bush along an animal trail and wait for someone to pass. Vibrations, shadows, and the gases in your breath get them excited. When they think a person is near, they frantically wave their front legs, hoping to grab you. Ticks don't jump or drop from the trees. That takes a bigger brain than any tick has.

Once a tick grabs you, it climbs up to your head or shoulders. A couple of hours later, it is drinking your blood. While it's drinking your blood, its mouth produces a liquid cement that glues the tick to your skin. It also produces a special fluid that freezes your skin and makes the bite painless so you can't feel anything. They might not have big brains, but ticks have all the tools they need to get a meal.

Twenty-four kinds of bats live in the prairies. Have you ever wondered how bats are different from birds? First of all, bats are mammals. That means they have fur instead of feathers and they drink milk, something a bird never does.

Secondly, bats never use a nest and they always have just one baby. Also, the naked baby bat often flies with its mother when she goes hunting at night, clinging to the fur on her chest like glue.

Thirdly, prairie bats always catch insects using the bare skin between their legs and tail that folds forward like a baseball mitt. Insect-eating birds, such as swallows, catch meals with their mouth.

Finally, birds and bats find insects at night in different ways. Most birds use their powerful eyes, whereas bats use their sensitive ears to listen for echoes. When a prairie bat is flying, it produces a rapid, clicking sound with its mouth that humans cannot hear. If the sound hits an insect, it bounces back and produces an echo that the bat can hear and follow.

These brown bats are huddled together in a cave where they are spending the cold months of winter.

THE CLEVER

COYOTE

This little deer mouse had climbed up a rose bush to feed on the juicy red fruits.

I have watched coyotes leaping after mice and ground squirrels in prairie river valleys. I have also seen them chasing cottontails in the badlands, running after songbirds out on the rolling grasslands, and sniffing for nesting ducks in the cattails around a pothole. The coyote is the largest predator living on the prairies today. At one time, there were wolves and grizzly bears on the prairies, but they disappeared many years ago.

The clever coyote is one of the most successful predators in all of North America. It not only lives in all of the wildlife habitats in the prairies, it also lives in deserts and in all the different forests that grow throughout the United States and Canada. I have even seen coyotes crossing the highways in big cities such as Hollywood, California.

Coyotes are able to live in so many different areas because they eat so many different kinds of foods. In the prairies, they hunt jackrabbits and cottontails in the winter and also eat any dead animals they happen to find. During bad winter blizzards many deer and pronghorn die, and sometimes cattle and sheep as well. These dead animals provide many meals for hungry coyotes. A coyote doesn't seem to mind if the meat is old, and it will even gobble up rotting meat that has maggots crawling on it.

MAGGOT: the worm-like period in the life of a fly

At other times of the year, coyotes eat whatever they can find, including snakes, lizards, toads, frogs, birds' eggs, mice, voles, muskrats, and insects. They will also nibble on berries, fruit, and seeds if the hunting is poor. To live for a year, the average coyote must catch about 75 jackrabbits, or around 160 cottontails. If it eats just mice and voles it must eat about 5,000 of them in a year. This is good news for farmers because the coyote destroys many small mammals that cause harm to crops.

The coyote was a favorite animal of Native Americans who once lived on the wide, open prairies. They admired the animal's cleverness and called it the "prairie trickster." Today, the coyote seems to be as tricky and clever as it always was. I'm happy about this because it means that the nighttime howling of these tricksters will be a wonderful part of the wild prairies for many years to come.

ECO-Alert

The forests that grow along the shores of many prairie rivers are flood forests. Each spring when the snow melts, the rivers overflow their banks and flood the forests. The floods are important because the muddy water brings food for the trees and helps them grow. However, dams have been built across many prairie rivers so they no longer overflow their banks in spring. As a result, prairie flood forests, and the wildlife they shelter, are slowly disappearing.

Wildlife lives in a different world than we do. It is a world we are only beginning to understand. I treasure the time I've spent observing nature in the prairies and around the world and learning its secrets. I remember the fun I had watching a playful swift fox pup chase a tumbleweed in the wind. I also remember my sense of amazement at seeing a mother grebe feeding her young a leech, and watching a ground squirrel with a bulging mouthful of grass as it prepared its winter nest. Most of all I will never forget the graceful flight of harriers courting above a prairie marsh or the excitement I felt as they suddenly dipped into the cattails, revealing their nest to me. I hope there will always be wild prairies for you to discover, where you can make wonderful memories of your own.

If you want to learn more about the prairies and the wildlife that lives there, you can search the Internet for the web sites I have listed below. This is where you can learn about the problems facing the prairies, what people are doing to save them, and how you can help.

Badlands National Park, South Dakota
www.nps.gov/badl/

Dinosaur Provincial Park
www.cd.gov.ab.ca/enjoying_alberta/parks/featured/dinosaur/
flashindex.asp

Ducks Unlimited
www.ducks.org/

Flint Hills, Kansas
http://flinthills.fws.gov/

Grasslands National Park, Saskatchewan
www.pc.gc.ca/pn-np/sk/grasslands/index_e.asp

National Bison Range, Montana
www.fws.gov/bisonrange/nbr/

National Parks and Conservation Association
www.npca.org/

Platte River, Nebraska
www.nature.org/wherewework/northamerica/states/nebraska/
preserves/art281.html

Theodore Roosevelt National Park, North Dakota
www.nps.gov/thro/

When DR. WAYNE LYNCH met AUBREY LANG,
he was an emergency doctor and she was a pediatric
nurse. Within five years they were married and had
left their jobs in medicine to work together as writers
and wildlife photographers. For twenty-seven years
they have explored the great wilderness areas of
the world—tropical rainforests, remote islands in the
Arctic and Antarctic, deserts, mountains, prairies,
and African plains.

Dr. Lynch is a popular guest lecturer and an
award-winning science writer. His books cover a wide
range of subjects, including the biology and behavior
of owls, penguins, and northern bears; arctic, boreal,
and grassland ecology; and the lives of prairie
birds and mountain wildlife. He is a fellow of the
internationally recognized Explorers Club, and an
elected Fellow of the prestigious Arctic Institute of
North America.

Dr. Lynch has written the texts and taken the
photographs for five other titles in NorthWord's
Our Wild World animal series: *Seals, Hawks, Owls,
Vultures,* and *Falcons.*